JOHN SCULLEY

Building

the

Apple Dream

JOHN SCULLEY

Building
the
Apple Dream

Harriet Spiesman

GEC GARRETT EDUCATIONAL CORPORATION

Cover: *John Sculley.* (Apple Computer.)

Manufactured in the United States of America

Edited and produced by Synthegraphics Corporation

Library of Congress Cataloging-in-Publication Data

Spiesman, Harriet, 1932-
   John Sculley : building the Apple dream / Harriet Spiesman.
     p. cm. — (Wizards of business)
   Includes index.
   Summary: A biography of John Sculley, who gave up the presidency of Pepsi-Cola to join Apple Computer, thus becoming one of America's most powerful corporate executives.
   ISBN 1-56074-023-X
   1. Sculley, John—Juvenile literature.   2. Apple Computer, Inc.—Juvenile literature.   3. Businessmen—United States—Biography—Juvenile literature.   4. Computer industry—United States—Juvenile literature. [1. Sculley, John. 2. Businessmen. 3. Apple Computer, Inc.]   I. Title. II. Series.
HD9696.C62S68   1991
338.7′61004165—dc20   91-28542
[B]   CIP
                                            AC

Contents

Chronology for **John Sculley**

1939	Born on April 6 in New York City
1960	Married Ruth Kendall
1961	Received bachelor's degree in architecture from Brown University
1963	Received master's degree in business administration from University of Pennsylvania
1965	Divorced Ruth Kendall
1967	Joined Pepsi-Cola as a trainee
1970	Became Pepsi's youngest marketing vice-president
1977	Steve Jobs and Steve Wozniak founded Apple Computer; John Sculley made president and chief executive officer of Pepsi-Cola
1978	Married Carol Lee ("Leezy") Adams
1983	Joined Apple Computer as president and chief executive officer
1986	Named chairman of Apple's board of directors in January
1991	Ranked third most powerful corporate executive in America by *Forbes* magazine

Chapter 1

Sugared Water or . . . ?

"Do you want to spend the rest of your life selling sugared water or do you want a chance to change the world?" It was March 1983. For months Steve Jobs, co-founder of Apple Computer, had been trying to persuade John Sculley to join Apple. This was an offer most men would jump at—to become the president and **chief executive officer** of one of the fastest growing companies in the country. (Terms in **boldface type** are defined in the Glossary at the back of this book.)

Sculley was tempted. He shared Steve Jobs' enthusiasm for new ideas and inventions. And John was fascinated by Steve's vision of how Apple could help shape the future. As the head of Apple,

John Sculley would be on the cutting edge of new computer technology. But it also meant giving up his fabulous career with Pepsi-Cola.

At age forty-three, John Sculley was already a rich and famous **executive.** In his sixteen years with PepsiCo, John had risen from a trainee to president of Pepsi-Cola, the company's soft-drink division. His salary that year was $500,000, and he was a likely candidate to replace Donald Kendall as chairman of PepsiCo's **board of directors.**

But Steve Jobs had captured John's imagination. John Sculley had always wanted to run a company and create new products. Now, Steve Jobs was offering him that opportunity. Computers certainly *were* more exciting than "sugared water"! However, John just wasn't sure he was ready to accept the challenge—and a whole new life-style.

A FORMAL UPBRINGING

John Sculley was born in New York City on April 6, 1939. His parents were John and Margaret (Blackburn) Sculley. John had two younger brothers, Arthur and David. Mr. Sculley was a prominent Wall Street lawyer with a Princeton education. He was devoted to his sons and determined to do everything possible to help them become successful.

The family lived a proper, formal life-style in a wealthy section of Manhattan, which is a part of New York City. John attended a private elementary day school for boys where he was required to wear a uniform that included a cap, jacket, shirt, and tie.

Early Years

When John was eleven years old, he was sent to St. Marks, which is a strict Episcopal boarding school for boys in Massachusetts. He attended chapel services twice daily, and followed a rigid schedule of classes and activities.

John was a painfully shy boy because he suffered from a severe stammer that made it difficult to complete a full sentence. In his autobiography, *Odyssey,* John discusses his stammer. "It drove me into a world of my own where I would fantasize about building my own car or conducting my own scientific experiments . . ." However, during his mid-teens, John's stammer was cured by medical hypnosis.

Instead of playing with toys, John would tinker with electrical gadgets. By the time he was ten, he and his friends had built remote-controlled robots out of old radio parts and Erector Sets. John's youngest brother, David, remembers wires and parts strewn all over the house.

John's grandfather was W.B. Smith, a Bermuda-born naval architect and engineer who shared John's enthusiasm for science and building things. John and his grandfather spent long hours together discussing space travel, scientific ideas, and W.B.'s World War II adventures.

Despite his stammer, John was an extremely successful student at St. Marks. He was elected president of his class for six consecutive years and served as captain of the school's soccer team. When John graduated, he was named "the senior boy who did the most for his class."

CHOOSING A CAREER

John's goal was to be an industrial designer. He wanted to skip college and go to art school. However, his father disapproved; he had hoped his son would follow in his footsteps and study law.

Eventually, John and his father reached a compromise. John would attend Brown University during the day and the Rhode Island School of Design at night. Both schools were in Providence, Rhode Island.

In 1960, while John was still at Brown, he met and married Ruth Kendall. Ruth's stepfather, Donald M. Kendall, was to become one of the most important people in John's life.

From Architecture to Marketing

John majored in art history and architecture at Brown, from which he graduated in 1961. He then continued studying architecture as a graduate student at the University of Pennsylvania.

One summer, while working as an **intern** for an industrial design firm, John made an important discovery. He realized that it was the people in **marketing,** not the designers, who had real power in the business world.

At the time, John's father-in-law, Don Kendall, was chairman of the board of directors at PepsiCo. He thought John had a talent for marketing, and encouraged him to switch from architecture to business, which John did.

In 1963, John received a master's degree in business administration (M.B.A.) from Wharton, the University of Pennsylvania's

Marketing

> Marketing involves all the activities necessary to move goods from a seller to a buyer. It includes advertising, promoting, and selling. Marketing people analyze the habits and preferences of **consumers.** They also study the competition.
>
> Marketing research shows if there is a demand for a product and how much the public is willing to pay. Marketing helps a company decide what new products to introduce and how to advertise them.

business school. At last he was ready to enter the world of business. John became a trainee at McCann-Erickson, a prominent advertising agency. Coca-Cola was their biggest client.

In those days, advertising agencies handled the marketing work for most companies. John worked on a secret marketing research project for Coke. Little did he know that this would be the beginning of his long involvement in the soft-drink industry.

By 1967, however, large companies were beginning to set up their own marketing departments. John wanted to join the marketing department of one of those companies.

Earlier, in 1965, John and his wife were divorced, but John had remained close to his father-in-law. When he told Don Kendall that he was looking for a job in marketing, Kendall suggested that he apply at PepsiCo.

In 1967, John Sculley became the first M.B.A. to work for Pepsi-Cola. It was the beginning of a career that would put him on the cover of *Business Week* magazine and earn him a reputation as a "genius at consumer marketing."

Chapter 2

Battling Coke

In 1886, a druggist in Atlanta, Georgia, mixed up the first batch of Coca-Cola. Twelve years later, in 1898, Caleb D. Bradham, a North Carolina druggist, developed Pepsi-Cola.

For the next eighty years, Coke remained the country's number-one selling soft drink with Pepsi trailing in second place. Coke, whose biggest advantage was its strong **image,** was more than just a popular beverage. It was a symbol of America, home, and family.

At Pepsi, the marketing department had one goal: to outsell Coke. Success was measured by **market share.** When John Sculley joined Pepsi in 1967, Coke was seven market-share points ahead of Pepsi-Cola. Each share point represented $100 million in sales.

STARTING AT THE BOTTOM

John spent his first six months at Pepsi in a training program. As a trainee, he sorted and washed bottles, drove delivery trucks, and arranged supermarket displays. However, John quickly discovered that he wasn't strong enough to haul the heavy cartons of bottles around. So, to build up his endurance and strength, he began running five miles a day and lifting weights.

When John completed the training program, he was assigned to marketing research. He was an energetic, tireless worker who thought nothing of working late into the night and straight through weekends.

His hard work paid off. In 1970, at the age of thirty, John was named Pepsi-Cola's vice-president of marketing, the youngest person ever to hold that position.

CORPORATE WAR ZONE

By 1970, Pepsi had been steadily losing ground in its battle to outsell Coke. Market shares had been down for the last four years, and the company resembled a war zone.

Pepsi-Cola executives were tough, sometimes ruthless, **competitors.** They drove themselves hard to gain market share and increase profits. Everyone was out to beat Coke; their jobs depended on it. The slightest shift in market-share figures could mean the end of someone's promising career.

John Sculley was eager to join this corporate battle as the new vice-president of marketing. He thrived on the competition and tension at Pepsi.

There were seventy-five men working in John's department. He was the youngest, yet he was the boss. John expected perfection from himself and everyone else.

John admits that he quickly earned a reputation for being impatient and insensitive. But he soon realized he had a lot to learn about managing people and building team spirit.

THE PEPSI GENERATION

John's first goal was to convince the public that Pepsi had a better image than Coke. Several years earlier, Pepsi had run an advertising campaign called the Pepsi Generation. John now decided to remake the commercials. They would show Pepsi as part of a new, exciting life-style.

John believed that marketing should be thought of as theater, like staging a performance. The way to get people interested in a product was to entertain them. So he hired Hollywood filmmakers to make commercials that were like miniature high-budget movies. No company had ever done this before, or spent so much on commercials.

The ads showed happy, attractive people enjoying themselves. They were based on the theme, "You've Got a Lot to Live and Pepsi's Got a Lot to Give." Viewers were told: "Drink Pepsi and enjoy the good life."

The Pepsi Generation campaign was a huge success. The commercials won awards and sales increased. John also made several other changes that improved business. He introduced new packaging and larger bottles that appealed to customers. As sales figures continued to climb, John Sculley was becoming a hero at the company.

PRESSURE TO SUCCEED

Each accomplishment made John determined to work even harder. Work was his whole life, and his life-style was very different from that of the older executives at Pepsi. They were family men who lived traditional suburban lives.

John did not have any home life. When he and Ruth were divorced in 1965, she and their children, Jack and Meg, moved to California. Later, a second marriage for John also ended in divorce.

In the formal business atmosphere of Pepsi, John's appearance was also unusual. He often wore desert boots with his suits and had to be reminded to get a haircut.

While at Pepsi, John was a loner, working long hours and existing on late-night pizza. His mind was constantly focused on business. He thought nothing of waking a fellow worker in the middle of the night to discuss a new idea.

Even on weekends, John would visit supermarkets with his youngest brother, David, who was also in marketing. Together, they would exchange ideas about packaging, advertising, and new products. John never stopped thinking about Pepsi's competitors.

Few people could please John. If someone didn't meet his high standards, John fired him and did the work himself. If that made him unpopular, it didn't matter. John Sculley was completely confident of his marketing ideas; he would do anything to put them to work.

AN INTERNATIONAL SUCCESS

In 1965, Pepsi-Cola Company merged with Frito-Lay to become PepsiCo. By 1973, PepsiCo was producing soft drinks, potato chips, pretzels, and other snack foods around the world. But Pepsi's International Foods operation was in trouble. It was the only division of the company that was losing money—$16 million a year.

John was put in charge of the international division. It was his job to turn the losses into **profits.** This was a challenge that no one else wanted, but John thought of it as a terrific adventure. He loved the idea of traveling around the world. And he especially looked forward to building a successful operation out of a loser.

A World Traveler

For 3½ years, John flew back and forth across the ocean every week with a hand-picked team of assistants. They closed some companies, set up new ones, and reorganized others.

At the end of the 3½ years, John and his team had turned the international division around. Instead of losing $16 million dollars a year, it was earning $40 million.

PRESIDENT OF PEPSI

As head of the international division, John was completely on his own. Life overseas was much more informal than back in the home office. No one in Spain or Brazil bugged him about his long hair!

John enjoyed his traveling adventures so much that twice he turned down the chance to become president of Pepsi. Finally, in 1977, he reluctantly agreed to become president and chief executive officer of the company.

One reason John decided to accept the promotion was that he had fallen in love with Carol Lee ("Leezy") Adams, a lively, independent woman from New York. They were married on March 7, 1978. Suddenly John Sculley had a new wife, a ten-year-old stepdaughter (Laura Lee), a dog, a cat, and two hamsters.

The Pepsi Challenge

As the president of Pepsi-Cola, Sculley was determined to push Pepsi ahead of Coke. Sales were improving, but Coke was still the leading soft drink. How could he make Pepsi number one?

John looked for the answer in market research. Studies showed that when people didn't know which cola they were drinking, they preferred the taste of Pepsi over Coke. If consumers were asked to choose the best drink from unmarked glasses, Pepsi was almost always the winner. However, if consumers were told in advance what they were drinking, they chose Coke.

The studies proved that Pepsi actually tasted better than Coke. This meant that many people were buying Coke because of its strong image, not for its taste. John realized this was information that Pepsi needed to get out to the public.

Under his leadership, Pepsi put together the "Pepsi Challenge" advertising campaign. The commercials showed ordinary people, not actors, taste-testing the two colas. The camera zoomed in on the people's surprised faces when they were told that they had chosen Pepsi over Coke.

Taste tests were held all over the country—in shopping malls, supermarkets, high school gyms, and on college campuses. The "Pepsi Challenge" was a huge success. Eventually, Pepsi sales moved ahead of Coke in the supermarkets. People were even saying that John Sculley was sure to be Donald Kendall's successor as the head of PepsiCo.

Then, just when John Sculley's future was brightest and his life seemed perfect, Steve Jobs offered him a job at Apple Computer.

Chapter 3

The Golden Apple

Shortly before Thanksgiving, 1982, John Sculley received a phone call from a well-known **headhunter.** Apple Computer was looking for a new chief executive. Steve Jobs and the people at Apple Computer knew about John's reputation as a marketing wizard and were eager to meet him.

"I know you don't want to leave Pepsi, and I hate to ask a favor of you," the headhunter told John. "But please trust me. Would you make a trip to California and at least meet these guys?"

John was scheduled to visit his children in California, so he agreed to include Apple in his travel plans. He was curious to see this new **high-tech** company everyone was talking about. You could hardly pick up a magazine without reading about Steve Jobs, the boy-wonder who founded Apple.

However, Sculley made it very clear to the headhunter. He would visit Apple, but he had no intention of considering a job offer.

John was just learning how to use his new office computer, an Apple II Plus. He knew very little about computers or the Apple company. John couldn't imagine leaving Pepsi-Cola for a computer company!

STEVE JOBS AND SILICON VALLEY

Steve Jobs and John Sculley came from two very different worlds. Sculley was the product of Ivy League schools (Harvard, Yale, Brown, etc.) and the buttoned-down corporate world. Jobs, on the other hand, was a college dropout—an electronics nut from California, land of sunshine, hot tubs, and Silicon Valley.

During the 1950s, silicon was one of the materials that created a revolution in communications systems. Slices of silicon, called chips, became the heart of computers. Chips contain devices that do the work of the computer.

Stanford University, near San Francisco, was located in the Santa Clara Valley region. For years, the university had attracted designers and engineers in the electronics industry. Hundreds of laboratories and factories sprang up in the area, and it soon became known as Silicon Valley.

A Weird Kid

As a young boy, Steve Jobs was a loner who loved electronics. He entered science fairs, hung out at electronics supply stores, and liked to discuss the meaning of life. Why are we here? Is there a God? He looked for the answers to such questions in Eastern religions like Zen Buddhism.

Steve had few friends in high school or college; he was considered weird. At Reed College in Portland, Oregon, he learned more about Zen Buddhism and decided he wanted to go to India.

Steve dropped out of college, worked for a while, and then took off for India. But by 1974, he was back home living with his parents. He landed a job at Atari, the video-game company.

After work, Steve would go to meetings of the Homebrew Computer Club. The members were researchers and engineers who worked at local companies. They would get together to share ideas and demonstrate new products.

At one of the club meetings, Jobs met an old friend, Steve Wozniak. "Woz," as he was called, was five years older than Steve, but they had common interests.

Starting a Business

Woz was a computer genius who had always dreamed of building a small computer of his own. As he talked about it and showed Jobs what he was doing, Steve became excited.

Constructing the computer was just a hobby for Woz. Steve, however, immediately saw it as a money-making opportunity. He persuaded Woz to quit his job at Hewlett-Packard so the two of them could go into business together.

Because they needed money for supplies, Steve sold his car and Woz sold his expensive calculator. With $1,300, they set up shop in the garage of Steve's parents.

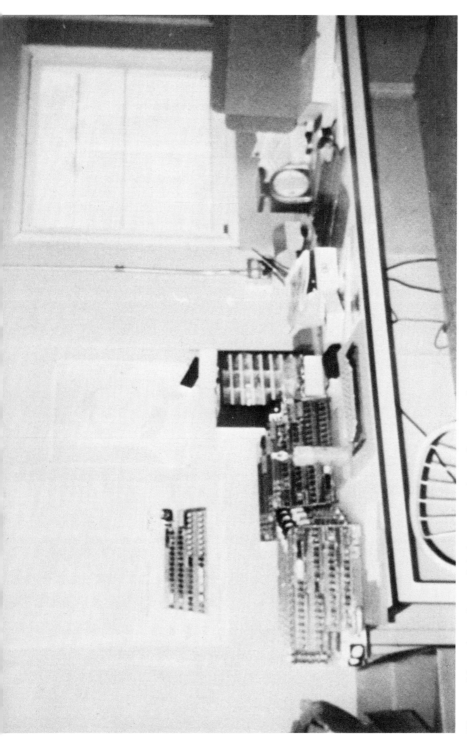

The workbench in Steve Jobs' garage where Steve and Woz assembled the first Apple computer. (Apple Computer, Inc.)

Steve and Woz named their new company Apple. Steve thought of the apple as the perfect fruit, a symbol of knowledge. Their company would produce the perfect computer.

THE COMPUTER REVOLUTION

In the 1950s, only large **corporations** or places like the Pentagon could afford computers. The first computers were too big and too costly for most people.

Early computers were called mainframes. They were fifteen feet long, nine feet tall, and usually weighed five tons. The mainframes were kept in dust-free, air-conditioned rooms. Highly trained experts were the only people able to operate these huge, complicated computers.

Ten years later, smaller machines, called minicomputers, became available. But they were also quite large. Computers remained big and expensive because the silicon chips used in them were big and expensive.

International Business Machines (IBM) built most of the early computers. It was and still is one of the largest and richest corporations in the world. IBM was the leader in computers at the time and has remained Apple's biggest competitor.

The First Apple

Steve Jobs and Woz formed Apple Computer in 1977. By then, researchers had figured out how to develop small silicon chips. Steve was convinced that he and Woz would now be able to produce a small computer.

The original Apple I computer. (Apple Computer, Inc.)

Instead of taking up a whole room, Apple would develop a small personal computer that would sit on a desktop. It would change the workplace forever. Jobs dreamed of putting computer power in the hands of ordinary people.

The first Apple Computer, Apple I, had no keyboard, no screen, and no case. It was sold unassembled, as a hobby kit, for the unusual price of $666.66. A local computer store, The Byte Shop, agreed to purchase a few dozen of the computers if they were preassembled.

Raising Money

By August 1976, Woz was designing a new model. It had a keyboard and was able to display color on a TV screen. While Woz worked on the computers, Steve Jobs frantically tried to raise money for their company. However, serious computer scientists didn't think personal computers had any value. And banks were reluctant to lend money to a 23-year-old man in ripped blue jeans.

Then Jobs was introduced to Mike Markkula, a wealthy, retired marketing manager. Because Markkula had faith in the new company, he put up $91,000 of his own money and arranged for a large bank loan. In return, Markkula became an equal partner and temporary chief executive of Apple Computer.

The company was now ready to move out of Steve's garage. For the first time, Apple began shipping to the mass market. The Apple II sold for $1,350 and earned profits of $139 million in the first three years it was on the market. In 1980, Apple became a public corporation.

Steve Wozniak (left) and Steve Jobs (right) proudly display the Apple I board. (Apple Computer, Inc.)

A Public Corporation

A corporation is a public company when its **stock** may be purchased by the general public. The total value of the company is divided into a certain number of equal shares of stock.

In order to sell its stock to the public, a company usually joins a stock exchange. Selling stock is a way for a company to raise **capital** so it can expand and become more profitable.

Individuals who buy stock (invest) in a company are called **shareholders.** If the company does well, the price of the stock rises; if the company does poorly, the price drops.

UPS AND DOWNS

From the beginning, Apple was run by two very different groups of people. Mike Markkula brought in experienced professionals who kept the business moving ahead.

Steve and Woz, on the other hand, were the "obsessed kids" with wild dreams and far-out ideas. They gathered around them a team of people like themselves. This team was young, long-haired, and bright. They felt special. It wasn't money they were after; they were at Apple to make a difference.

Steve Jobs was the man who could fire up anybody. He could convince you black was white, up was down, and forget he ever said

Apple Computer's first corporate headquarters in Silicon Valley. (Apple Computer, Inc.)

it the next day. It was Markkula and his more practical-minded people who kept Steve more or less under control.

A BEEHIVE OF ACTIVITY

Apple was an undisciplined beehive of activity. Under Mike Markkula's temporary leadership, 1980 was a boom year for the company.

The Apple II made millionaires of hundreds of employees who owned stock in the company. People often said Apple was run by kids with money falling out of their jeans. The parking lot looked like a car dealership for Mercedes or Porsche.

Despite the company's initial success, Apple's next two computers were flops. The Apple II Plus sold poorly, and the Apple III was a total disaster. Its chips failed, parts shorted out, cables were too short—the list of problems kept growing. Unfortunately, these failures gave competitors like the new IBM PC a chance to catch up to the Apple II.

In spite of these setbacks, the Apple II continued to keep the company enormously successful. Sales in 1982 were $583.1 million. Within five years of its founding, Apple Computer was a **Fortune 500** company.

Mike Markkula now felt that the time had come for him to step down as temporary chief executive. He recognized that the company had reached a point where it badly needed a strong business and marketing manager—someone like John Sculley.

Chapter 4

"I Just Have a Feeling"

Sunday, December 19, 1982, was a day full of surprises for John Sculley. Driving out to Cupertino, California, John expected to find Apple Computer located in a sleek, high-tech setting. This was, after all, Silicon Valley, the center of new computer technology.

Instead, compared to other companies in the Valley, Apple looked pretty ordinary. It consisted of an odd assortment of wooden buildings. To reach Mike Markkula's office, John was told he'd have to climb an outside stairway to the second floor!

SCULLEY MEETS JOBS

Sculley spent the day soaking up the excitement generated by the Apple staff. It was a crowded, noisy place. There were no private offices, just open cubicles packed close together. Dozens of printers banged away while the phones never stopped ringing.

Most of the Apple people were young, in their early twenties. John was the only man wearing a suit. Blue jeans seemed to be the standard uniform. Steve Jobs' office was cluttered with electronics parts and products he had taken apart to examine.

"We've got some incredible ideas that will revolutionize the way people use computers," Steve told John. "We're going to be doing something that is really going to blow everybody's mind with a neat new product." He was referring to their newest computer design, the Lisa.

Steve wanted John to join Apple for several reasons. He knew Sculley was a real marketing whiz. Steve had no business skills and wanted to learn from an expert. And John was a gadget person. He loved figuring out how things worked and how they could be improved.

They hit it off right away. John was turned on by what he saw at Apple. He was especially intrigued by Steve's brilliant mind.

Even though Sculley wasn't ready to consider the job, he gave Steve some helpful marketing suggestions.

Keeping Up the Pressure

For the next few months, Jobs kept up the pressure to win John over to Apple. Steve wasn't the type to take no for an answer. He kept up a barrage of phone calls, visits to New York, and long, intimate talks.

John Sculley and Steve Jobs were very much alike. They were both ambitious, impatient people who set extremely high standards for themselves and others. They understood each other and quickly developed a close friendship.

Once John asked Steve why he wasn't looking for someone experienced in computers. Steve explained, " . . . we've got to be a great marketing company. You really understand marketing. . . . I just have a feeling that this could be very important for all of us."

John was tempted. This was an opportunity to build a young company and to share the adventure with brilliant, creative people.

Also, taking the job would let John fulfill his boyhood dream—a career in electronics. Everyone seemed to have fun at Apple. That certainly wasn't the case in the formal, competitive atmosphere at Pepsi.

And if he moved to California, John would be closer to his children, Jack and Meg. Now, in order to be with them, he flew back and forth across the country every three weeks.

MAKING A TOUGH DECISION

Leaving Pepsi-Cola would be a tremendous career gamble for John Sculley. What if he accepted the job at Apple and it didn't work out? Today, John Sculley could have just about any job he wanted in the corporate world. That certainly wouldn't be true if he failed at Apple.

Was it fair to expect his wife and stepdaughter to move from one end of the country to the other? Was he being disloyal to the people at Pepsi who had been like his family?

John had confidence in his marketing ability, but he wondered if he was crazy to think he could switch from soft drinks to a totally different industry.

Overcoming the Obstacles

John finally told Steve what it would take for him to leave Pepsi: $1 million a year in salary, an additional $1 million bonus the first year, and $1 million if he was forced to resign from Apple. He also insisted that Apple help him buy a new home in California.

Apple accepted John's terms and included valuable **stock options.** With this kind of security, John knew his family would be well protected.

Breaking the news to Don Kendall, Pepsi's chief, wasn't easy. But Kendall and John's other co-workers realized he'd be out of his mind to turn down such a generous offer.

Adjusting to Change

The Apple executive staff met their new leader for the first time on April 13, 1983. There were a dozen or so vice-presidents at Apple, and they were uneasy. John Sculley was practically a foreigner. He knew virtually nothing about the computer industry.

For John, the new company was a dramatic change from PepsiCo. Pepsi's headquarters in New York's Westchester County resembled a stately English manor home. The offices were elegant, and Pepsi employees were treated to lovely art and sculpture. The only artworks at Apple were slogan T-shirts and posters taped to the walls.

Apple wasn't like companies where the boss gives orders and everyone obeys. At Apple, everyone was encouraged to give opinions and ideas. Meetings were informal and often turned into shouting matches.

Sculley welcomed the enthusiasm and pride of those around him. He enjoyed the casual atmosphere and traded in his suits for khakis and sport shirts. John felt better than he had in years as he plunged into his new career.

Chapter 5

Learning the Ropes

When John arrived at Apple in the spring of 1983, business was booming. The company couldn't fill orders fast enough.

Apple's extraordinary growth had made its founders overnight celebrities. The media created folk heroes out of the new millionaires in blue jeans. Steve Jobs appeared on the cover of *Fortune* magazine. He was hailed as a quirky young genius in the world of **entrepreneurs.**

THE APPLE ORGANIZATION

In reality, however, Steve and Woz provided the dream and the creative ideas. Mature, experienced business people like Mike Markkula and John Sculley were responsible for the long-term growth of Apple Computer. Steve and his young followers at Apple were undisciplined risk takers, and they were totally committed to Steve's vision of the future.

Jobs was Apple's largest shareholder and chairman of the board of directors. But he was not trained in business or engineering, and was never an equal partner in running the company. There were even times when Steve interfered in engineering decisions and annoyed department managers. From the beginning, Mike and the other business professionals knew they had to control Steve's recklessness.

Hard-Working Employees

Steve's biggest contribution to Apple was his dynamic personality and his ability to motivate people. The average worker in the United States works about 40 hours a week. But Steve inspired people to put in from fifty to ninety hours a week. Apple employees proudly wore T-shirts that read, "Working 50 hours a week and loving it!"

When John took over at Apple, he came in as president and chief executive officer. Steve remained vice-president and chairman of the board of directors. It was understood from the start that Steve would be working under John's direction.

An Inseparable Team

The two men were anxious to learn from each other. Sculley wanted to know as much as possible about computers. The person he listened to most was Steve, who depended on John to teach him marketing skills.

They admired each other and soon became an inseparable team. Although John was supposed to be in charge, he began sharing more and more power with Steve. John would later realize that this was a major mistake.

A SHAKY FUTURE

Apple Computer had a record year in 1983, when the company's sales reached $982 million. But the situation was rapidly changing. Low-cost computers like Atari were in trouble. Some computer companies were even forced out of business in the 1980s. The future looked shaky for the entire computer industry, and John Sculley identified several problems at Apple.

During the past few years, the public's fascination with computers had slowed down. The novelty of computers was wearing off. The Apple IIe (an improved version of the Apple II) sold for $1,400. But consumers were beginning to question the wisdom of spending that much money just to balance a checkbook or play computer games.

Also, IBM, Apple's strongest competitor, was coming out with a new personal computer (PC). For this reason, many parents held off buying computers for their children. They wanted a chance to see the new IBM first.

A Disappointing Office Computer

IBM was also the leading manufacturer of office computers. Apple, however, was counting on its most powerful computer, the redesigned Lisa, to break IBM's hold on office computers.

Unfortunately, the Lisa sales were disappointing. It was an expensive computer, costing $10,000, and business people complained that it was too slow and very difficult to use. More important, the Lisa wasn't **compatible** with IBM computers.

Customers wanted new computers that could share information with their IBM machines and run the same **software.** But John and Steve didn't accept the idea that Apple had to be IBM-compatible in order to succeed.

Nevertheless, the issue came up again and again. Should Apple computers be redesigned to make them IBM-compatible? Sculley and Jobs continued to think that Apple should remain independent. They insisted that Apple built quality products good enough to stand on their own.

Tightening Up

One of the first things Sculley did when he joined Apple was to cut back on expenses. Apple had been hiring an average of 250 new employees every month. The huge staff was costing too much and John saw no need for it. He reduced hiring to zero.

Sculley also eliminated the company's **profit-sharing** program. This upset many employees, but he saw it as a necessary cut-back.

TAKING A BITE OUT OF APPLE

IBM had always been the leader in the business market with its mainframes and minicomputers. Apple, on the other hand, had been the leading manufacturer of personal computers. Now all that was changing.

As soon as IBM started selling its PC, it became Apple's biggest rival. By late 1983, IBM's PC sales were neck and neck with

Apple. *Business Week* ran a cover story in October and named IBM the winner in the **microcomputer** race. Sculley was furious.

Resisting Change

Advisors were urging Apple to redesign its computers and start building IBM **clones,** which a number of computer companies were already doing. To follow their lead, Apple would have to change its **operating system** and adopt MS-DOS, the IBM operating system.

Sculley and Jobs resisted taking such a drastic step. It would mean giving up everything they stood for. The company had been established to change the way people live and work with computer technology. For Apple to remain a leader in this technology, they must use their own system, not IBM's.

Meanwhile, a small division at Apple was experimenting with an exciting new computer design. John Sculley decided to pin the company's future on this new computer, the Macintosh.

Chapter 6

The Mighty Mac

At first, people at Apple didn't pay much attention to the Macintosh project. All the company's efforts were directed toward the Apple II and Lisa divisions.

The Mac team began as a small group of free-thinking, creative artists. They met in a building half a mile from Apple headquarters.

But more than distance separated them from the rest of the company. The Mac team thought the Lisa was a really a fouled-up machine. They would do things differently and build a much better computer.

DEVELOPING A USER-FRIENDLY PC

Steve Jobs had always resented the fact that he wasn't permitted to take charge of the Lisa project, so he started hanging around the Mac group. The more Steve learned about the Macintosh, the more involved he became. The group idolized him. Gradually, Steve took control of the project.

This was a group that thrived on excitement. Before long they were calling themselves "Steve's Pirates." Determined to revolutionize personal computers, they grabbed ideas, parts, and people from other divisions. In fact, they took whatever they needed to build their dream computer.

Once during a meeting, one member of the Mac team got up and said, " . . . for us in the Macintosh group, the product is like— it's like this torch being carried into a pitch-black room. . . . We like to say that it's incredibly, insanely great."

Until then, all personal computers were difficult to use. People had to spend hours learning how to operate one. Designers of the Macintosh wanted it to have simple instructions. This computer would be user-friendly, easy for anyone to operate.

Borrowing a Mouse

Certain features made the Macintosh special. Some of these features were borrowed from other Apple products. The Mac, like Lisa, used a "mouse" to point to a spot on the screen.

The mouse was a small box that could fit in one's hand. When it was moved across a desktop, a pointer moved in the same direction on the screen. Clicking a button on the mouse sent a command to the computer.

Another Macintosh feature was the use of simple pictures, called icons, to represent commands. Icons were easier to understand than word commands that had to be written in complicated computer terms.

Mac was also the first computer to use a 3½-inch **disk drive** instead of the standard 5¼-inch drive. The smaller disk was safer, sturdier, and could store more information.

INTRODUCING MAC

Up to this time, there had been two milestones in the history of personal computers: the Apple II and the IBM PC. Macintosh was really different; it would be the third milestone. John Sculley wanted its introduction to be treated as a major event.

John decided to turn the event into a "two-horse race" between IBM and Apple. He directed an advertising campaign based on George Orwell's book, *1984*.

An Award-Winning Commercial

A 60-second television commercial was broadcast during the Super Bowl game in January 1984. Without ever mentioning IBM by name, it showed "Big Brother" (IBM) trying to control the world. Good old user-friendly Macintosh rushed in and saved the day!

It was a startling, dramatic presentation with thundering sound and explosions of light. The last words spoken were, "On January 24th, Apple Computer will introduce Macintosh. (Pause) 1984 won't be like *1984*."

When it aired, the commercial caused a sensation. Television stations, newspapers, and magazines ran stories about Apple's innovative ad. *Advertising Age* magazine named John Sculley "Ad Man of the Year." The *1984* commercial won dozens of awards, including a prize at the Cannes Film Festival.

Millions of people saw or heard about the commercial. In less than three months, Apple sold 50,000 Macs. It took IBM over seven months to sell that many PCs.

In 1983, Steve Jobs (left) and John Sculley (right) introduced the Macintosh computer. (Apple Computer, Inc.)

Apple spent $15 million to introduce the Mac. This made it one of the largest advertisers in the United States. Originally, the Macintosh was supposed to sell for $1,000. But advertising costs pushed the price to $2,495.

At about the same time, Sculley launched the new Apple IIc, a portable version of the Apple II. The IIc was light in weight and half as expensive as the Mac.

FAME AND FORTUNE

The Mac and Apple IIc sold faster than expected. Apple's **revenues** for fiscal year 1984 were over $1.5 billion, and the company was elected to the Consumers Digest Hall of Fame.

Fiscal Year

A fiscal year is any twelve-month period used to settle or report financial (money) matters. A business, government, or other organization establishes its own fiscal year.

The fiscal year (FY) of the United States government begins on October 1. At Apple, the fiscal year also begins on October 1 and ends twelve months later, on September 30. Thus, Apple's fiscal year 1992 refers to the period beginning on October 1, 1991, and ending on September 30, 1992.

In October 1984, *Business Week* magazine ran a story about John Sculley and Steve Jobs. They were pictured on the cover as the "Dynamic Duo." President Ronald Reagan made jokes about Apple. Lee Iacocca, the chairman of Chrysler Corporation, visited Sculley and praised Apple's astounding success.

However, John's family paid a price for his sudden fame. There were death threats and a kidnapping attempt against John.

One day when John was jogging near his house, he spotted a car hidden behind some shrubbery. Suddenly two men leaped out and ran after him. John managed to get home safely. But for two months bodyguards stayed at the house.

A Good Year for Everyone

In spite of the kidnapping attempt, it had been a good year for John, for Steve Jobs, and for the company. John said he'd never made a decision he felt better about than the one that brought him to Apple.

Steve Jobs celebrated John's first year at Apple by throwing a party. He said, "This has been the greatest year I've ever had in my whole life because I've learned so much from John."

Sculley and Jobs were close friends and partners in an adventure to make Apple Computer a "phenomenally great company." What could possibly happen to split apart this "Dynamic Duo"?

Chapter 7

Shake-up and Turnaround

Apple ended its fiscal year 1984 with high hopes for continuing growth. But just four months later, John Sculley was facing serious problems.

John had been way too optimistic about future sales. He had recommended building up a huge **inventory** of computers, but sales lagged. Now millions of dollars were tied up in unsold products.

Critics complained that the Mac wasn't powerful enough; it had only one disk drive and too little memory. Apple had promised new business software and a network system (AppleTalk) for the Mac. But the Macintosh division was unable to meet delivery dates.

John realized that he had relied on Steve Jobs too much. Steve was an inspiring leader, but a poor business manager. He also could be arrogant and a bully.

WARRING DIVISIONS

Jobs had created destructive rivalry between his Mac team and the rest of the company. Having always insisted that the Macintosh people were the best in the company, he and his group began calling everyone else "Bozos."

But despite the Mac's early success, the Apple II division was still Apple's biggest moneymaker. Apple II people complained, however, that Sculley listened to Jobs too much and neglected their division in favor of Macintosh. Woz, one of Apple's founders and designer of the Apple II, resigned in disgust.

Bad news continued into 1985. Key executives and engineers lost faith in Apple and left the company.

A CRUMBLING FRIENDSHIP

For the first time, John Sculley and Steve Jobs were openly disagreeing. Wherever he turned, John found conflicts created by Steve. Even people in the Mac group began complaining about Steve's mismanagement.

There were also several occasions when John believed Steve had ruined business opportunities for the company with his reckless comments. "Who's really running this company anyway?" someone asked John. "If you're running the company, why is Steve Jobs . . . telling us all what to do?"

Painful Changes

Things were getting so bad that John realized he would have to remove Steve as manager of the Macintosh division. He told Steve he wanted him to continue as chairman of the board and focus on new technologies and products. At the same time, John would reorganize the Mac division and work through the company's present problems.

On April 10, 1985, the board of directors backed John's recommendations. Steve Jobs was furious. He said John would destroy the company, that John was a big part of Apple's problems.

Steve was moved out of the Macintosh building. He continued as chairman of the board, but he had no management authority.

It was a painful way to end a valued friendship. John felt sick to his stomach. But he knew his responsibility to the company was more important than personal feelings.

REORGANIZATION AT APPLE

Sculley acknowledged that both he and Jobs had created problems for Apple. Now he was determined to undo the damage. John eliminated the quarreling Apple and Macintosh divisions and created one manufacturing department and one marketing division.

Because Apple was still sitting with large inventories, John was forced to close three factories and lay off 1,200 employees. Since his days at Pepsi, however, he'd become a lot more sensitive about firing people. He set up a well-equipped center for the fired employees to use, and he hired consultants to help them find new jobs.

John blamed himself for the mistakes that caused the layoffs. One of John's mistakes was spending too much money on advertising and not enough on research and development of new products. He vowed to make product development a top priority.

Next, Inc.

In September 1985, Steve Jobs announced to the board of directors that he was resigning from Apple. He was starting his own computer company called Next, Inc. Five key Apple employees would be going with him.

It was obvious to Sculley that Jobs was going to use Apple technology to build his new computer. To prevent this, Apple began a law suit that was settled a year later. Steve would be allowed to build computers if Next, Inc., agreed not to use Apple trade secrets or compete with Apple products

APPLE POLISHING

One of John's best decisions was to bring Woz back to Apple. This was a move that boosted everyone's morale. Woz was one of the founders of the company and had always been well-liked and respected.

Sculley also insisted that to improve sales, the company must develop technology that would allow Apple computers to plug into other computer networks. This was a move that Steve Jobs and his followers had stubbornly resisted.

The ability to network with IBM and other computers helped increase Apple's share of the business market. Apple also successfully launched the Apple IIGS to replace older Apple II models. The IIGS offered superior **graphics** and sound.

The company was beginning to rebound. In a vote of confidence, John Sculley was named chairman of Apple's board of directors in January 1986.

Desktop Publishing

One of Apple's most popular new products was software and hardware for desktop publishing. This allowed a company or individual to design and print newsletters, reports, or even books on a personal computer. Desktop publishing saves the time and expense of using an outside printing firm.

Low-Cost Macs

IBM-compatibles were slashing computer prices. When customers complained that a Macintosh cost twice as much as an IBM clone, John ordered changes that lowered the cost of the Mac and made it more competitive.

Eventually, there were six Macintosh models. Some were discontinued as newer technology was developed. A new operating system for the Mac, System 7, was released in May 1991. A computer columnist rated it, "The best, most complete, and most compelling computer operating system you can buy."

APPLE'S FUTURE

While John was struggling to improve Apple's operations in the United States, Michael Spindler, Apple's chief executive in Europe, tripled the company's European sales. In January 1990, John decided to bring Spindler to the United States as Apple's chief operating officer.

Spindler became Sculley's number-two man. He took over operating responsibilities while John took control of product devel-

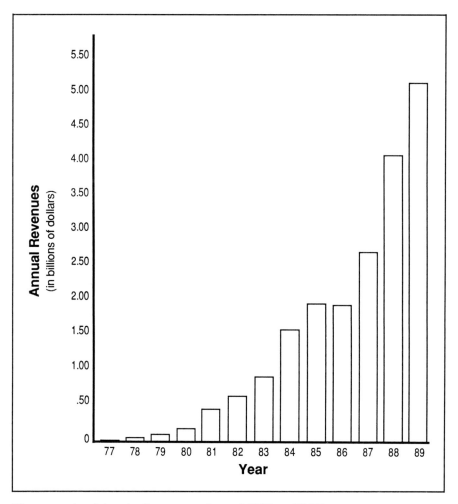

The growth of Apple Computer from 1977 to 1989.

opment. But there were many people who didn't think John had enough background in technology to run the product development department. He proved them wrong, however.

John continues to make product development his top priority. He envisions the development of a portable device called a Personal Intelligent Communicator that will include the features of personal computers, beepers, and cellular telephones.

Sculley admits that Apple missed the boat by not coming out early with a laptop computer. However, he promises to have a notebook computer ready in the very near future. It will be battery operated and about the size of an 8½ by 11-inch notebook.

Moving into Japan

In its May 27, 1991, issue, *Forbes* magazine listed 800 of corporate America's most powerful executives. John Sculley was ranked third. At age fifty-two, after eight years as chief executive officer of Apple, John's salary plus stock gains totaled over $16 million for the year. Apple sales were over $5 billion and profits topped $5 million.

An article about John Sculley appeared in the same issue of *Forbes*. The article was titled, "How Apple Stormed Japan" and praised the company's performance.

"Any computer company that wants to be a leader by the end of the century has to have an important business in Japan," John told *Forbes*. Sculley is well on his way toward achieving that goal.

In 1989, John hired a Japanese executive from Toshiba to become president of Apple Japan. Under Shigechika Takeuchi's leadership, Macintosh computers are springing up all over that country. The editor of *Nikkei Personal Computering,* Japan's leading computer magazine, said that the Mac is easier to use than Japanese computers!

The all-in-one design of the Apple Macintosh Portable computer makes it an easy to-carry package. (Apple Computer, Inc.)

BACK TO THE FUTURE

John Sculley met plenty of resistance with each change he made at Apple. Now, thanks to his leadership, Apple executives say no idea is off limits and no rule is unbreakable.

John says that both he and the company thrive on crisis. He's had his share, and he has managed to lead Apple out of crisis to a position of strength in the computer industry.

In his book, *Odyssey,* John wrote, "I sometimes think of where the world was before Apple began . . . and how far we've come. . . . It's as if we already are a twenty-first century company that has miraculously . . . come back to the late twentieth century to make sure we don't fail or compromise our mission along the way."

Glossary

board of directors   A group of people who run the affairs of a company for those who own stock in it.

capital   Money, goods, or property that can be used to make more goods or money.

chief executive officer (CEO)   A company's highest ranking decision-maker.

clone   A copy or reproduction having the same features as the original.

compatible   Able to get along with. For example, an IBM-compatible computer is one with the same operating system as an IBM and able to run IBM software.

competitor   Persons or organizations that are rivals, as in business.

consumers   Those who buy and use products.

corporation   A group of people formed to carry on a business enterprise, with legally given rights and duties.

disk drive   A computer device that reads, writes, and stores information on a magnetic disk.

entrepreneur   A person who organizes, manages, and assumes the risks of a business.

executive   A person who manages or helps to manage the affairs of a company or other organization.

Fortune 500   The 500 U.S. companies with highest sales, according to *Fortune* magazine.

graphics   Images or designs; or, as in computing, the ability to display them.

headhunter   A person who specializes in finding executives or other employees for companies.

high-tech   The most advanced scientific equipment and engineering methods.

image   Public opinion of a person or an organization.

intern   An advanced student or graduate working as an assistant under the supervision of someone with more experience.

inventory   Supply of goods or products on hand.

marketing The advertising and selling of products or services by companies.

market share The amount of sales an individual company has made of a product in relation to the entire amount of sales by all manufacturers of that product; usually calculated per year and expressed as a percentage.

microcomputer Small, relatively inexpensive computer; also known as a personal or home computer.

operating system The essential computer software that manages everything in memory and keeps track of information going to the disk drive, printer, screen, or other component of the computer.

profit The money left over from selling goods or services after subtracting expenses.

profit sharing A plan under which employees share in the profits of a business.

revenues Income or money obtained from sales.

shareholders Those who own shares of stock in a company; also called stockholders.

software The programs (information and instructions) used to run computers.

stock A certificate of ownership in a company.

stock options The right to buy a certain number of shares of stock in a company at a fixed price (usually lower than the selling price on the open market).

Index